GW01553281

national **TESTS**
practice papers

FOR THE YEAR **2002**

English

practice Papers

AGE
13-14
Key Stage 3

Ray Barker

Christine Moorcroft

Acknowledgements

The authors and publisher would like to thank the following for permission to reproduce material in this book.

The Daydreamer by Ian McEwan, Jonathon Cape Ltd, 1994
Cats and Kittens, RSPCA Animal Care, 1992
A High Wind in Jamaica, Richard Hughes, Harvill Press, 1994

Every effort has been made to trace and acknowledge ownership of copyright material but if any have been inadvertently overlooked, the publisher will be pleased to make the necessary alterations at the first opportunity.

First published 2001
exclusively for WHSmith by

Hodder & Stoughton Educational,
a division of Hodder Headline Ltd
338 Euston Road
London NW1 3BH

Text © Hodder & Stoughton Educational 2001

A CIP record for this book is available from the British Library.

Authors: Christine Moorcroft and Ray Barker
Series editor: Louis Fidge
Illustrations:

ISBN 0340 84593 7

Typeset by Dorchester Typesetting Group Ltd
Printed and bound by Graphycems, Spain

NOTE: The tests, questions and advice in this book are not reproductions of the official test materials sent to schools. The official testing process is supported by guidance and training for teachers in setting and marking tests and interpreting the results. The results achieved in the tests in this book may not be the same as are achieved in the official tests.

Contents

The National Tests: A Summary

What are the National Tests?

Children who attend state schools in England and Wales sit National Tests (also known as SATs) at the ages of 7, 11 and 14, usually at the beginning of May. The test results are accompanied by an assessment by the child's teacher (at Key Stage 3 this also covers non-tested subjects such as History or Geography). The results are used by the school to assess each child's level of knowledge and progress in English and Maths at Key Stage 1 and English, Maths and Science at Key Stages 2 and 3. They also provide useful guidance for the child's next teacher when he or she is planning the year's work.

The educational calendar for children aged 5-14 is structured as follows:

Key Stage	Year	Age by end of year	National Test
1 (KS1)	1	6	
	2	7	KEY STAGE 1
2 (KS2)	3	8	Optional Year 3
	4	9	Optional Year 4
	5	10	Optional Year 5
	6	11	KEY STAGE 2
3 (KS3)	7	12	
	8	13	
	9	14	KEY STAGE 3

Timetable

The Key Stage 1 National Tests are carried out in **May**. Key Stage 2 tests take place in one week in May. All children sit the same test at the same time. In 2002, the tests will take place in the week of **13-17 May**.

Key Stage 3 students will sit their tests on **7-13 May 2002**, with the following timetable (check with your school as details may change):

Tuesday 7 May	Wednesday 8 May	Thursday 9 May	Friday 10 May	Monday 13 May
MORNING				
English Paper 1 (1½ hours plus 15 minutes reading time)	Mathematics Paper 1 (1 hour)	English Extension Paper (1½ hours)	Science Paper 1 (1 hour)	Science Extension Paper (1 hour)
	Mental Arithmetic Tests A and C (20 minutes)	Mental Arithmetic Test B (20 minutes)		
AFTERNOON				
English Paper 2 (1¼ hours)	Mathematics Paper 2 (1 hour)	Mathematics Extension Paper (1 hour)	Science Paper 2 (1 hour)	

Levels

National average levels have been set for children's results in the National Tests. The levels are as follows:

LEVEL	AGE 7 (Key Stage 1)	AGE 11 (Key Stage 2)	AGE 14 (Key Stage 3)
8			
7			
6			
5			
4			
3			
2			
2a			
2b			
2c			
1			

- BELOW EXPECTED LEVEL
- EXPECTED LEVEL
- ABOVE EXPECTED LEVEL
- EXCEPTIONAL

Results

Your child's school will send you a report indicating his or her levels in the tests and the teacher assessment.

The school's overall test results will be included in local and national league tables, which are published in most newspapers.

What can parents do to help?

While it is never a good idea to encourage cramming, you can help your child to succeed by:

- Making sure he or she has enough food, sleep and leisure time during the test period.
- Practising important skills such as writing and reading stories, spelling and mental arithmetic.
- Telling him or her what to expect in the test, such as important symbols and key words.
- Helping him or her to be comfortable in test conditions, including working within a time limit, reading questions carefully and understanding different ways of answering.

English at Key Stage 3

In English pupils are required to sit two test papers.

Paper 1

Time allowed: 1 hour 30 minutes plus 15 minutes reading time

Section A – a test of reading based on a narrative or descriptive piece.

Section B – a test of reading based on an information text or on a poem.

Section C – a test of writing. Several options are given: writing a story, writing an argument or expressing a personal point of view.

Paper 2

Time allowed: 1 hour 10 minutes

This is based on the study of a Shakespeare play at Key Stage 3. For 2002 the choices are **Henry V**, **Twelfth Night** and **Macbeth.**

A booklet containing printed versions of scenes from the play is provided. A copy of the entire text is not permitted.

Two questions are set on different scenes and each pupil must choose one of these for which to supply an answer.

Marking the papers

Papers are marked by external examiners according to a strict set of criteria. In this way a national consensus can be achieved which is much fairer to all candidates. Each pupil is awarded a final score for the whole English test. This will equate to a National Curriculum level.

Paper 1

Section A is marked simply for the understanding of the passage set. This is judged by reading and writing tasks although the way in which the answers are written is not assessed.

Section B is marked for the ability to understand and describe the author's intention – how the author intended to influence the reader. Again, this is judged by reading and writing tasks although the way in which the answers are written is not assessed.

Section C is marked for the ability to be able to write and communicate ideas. The style of writing does matter here as do the quality of ideas and grammatical features such as sentence structure, spelling, punctuation and grammar.

The mark scheme will vary from year to year for this paper but it will generally be worth about 60 marks.

Paper 2

This paper on a Shakespeare play is marked for:

- **Understanding and response** – an understanding of Shakespeare's meaning and intention.

- **Written expression** – an ability to write clearly using features such as sentence structure, spelling, punctuation and grammar.

The mark scheme will vary from year to year for this paper but it will generally be worth about 40 marks.

How to help your child

Tests and exams can be very stressful. This is mostly because people do not like to feel 'judged' by others. Try sitting one yourself to find out what it feels like!

The tests in this book are modelled as closely as possible on the 'real thing' so pupils will not be surprised by the test format. However, you can help with the pressure of the tests by using the material in this book as a resource for teaching and learning. Share the experiences, questions and discussion that arise from the tests.

What can I do?

- Choose a comfortable, secure environment in which to do the tests together.

- Provide plenty of lined paper for your child.

- Talk about each of the questions and possible ways forward.

- Stick to the time limits – but do not insist that the entire test paper has to be completed in one go.

- Mark the work together, praising positive points as well as pointing out things which are not correct.

- Look closely at how the incorrect responses can be corrected, what needs to be learned or changed and how this can be done realistically. It is useful to list just two or three things which need to be done or learned before the next test session.

- Give immediate feedback – do not wait too long to discuss the performance of the candidate.

- Be positive about achievements.

- Use the experience gained from this book to help your child to go on to improve their performance.

- If you are concerned about your child ask his or her teacher for advice.

Advice to students on sitting the tests

- Look at the entire test paper first to establish what has to be done. Highlight the time restraints and the number of questions which need to be answered.

- Read the questions carefully. Underline key words, e.g. 'compare', 'two reasons…'. Be relevant in your answers.

- Make notes on the test paper. Underline important points and circle or highlight information relevant to the question.

- Make notes before you start to write. You only get the one chance so think about what you want to write before you put your pen to paper.

- Follow the help given on the paper. If the examiners have given a list of points to follow then use these as the plan for your work.

- Pace yourself – keep an eye on the clock.

- Which question is worth more marks? Spend more time on that question – but not too much more time. Write the time you need to spend on each of the questions by the side of them on the question paper.

- Look at how many marks are allocated. Try to make that many points. If there are 8 marks, make 8 points (and back them up with evidence from the text).

- When you write your answer, write in sentences. Don't be afraid to cross things out and write them again.

- Write in paragraphs (you could leave a line between them) – this makes your work easier to read.

- Use quotations – but not huge chunks! Use them to back up your points. It is best to quote short phrases and single words.

- You will be given good marks if your use of grammar, spelling and punctuation helps to make your meaning clear.

- If you get stuck on a question, leave it for the moment – but remember to leave a page empty in your answer book in case you want to go back.

- Look at the checklist below to help you answer the questions properly.

- If you have time left, go back over your answers.

Features to consider

Paragraphs
Is my work divided into paragraphs so that the examiner can see when I stop writing about one aspect and start writing about another? This is an important stylistic feature and helps you communicate your message clearly to the examiner.

Quotations
Are my quotations too long?
Have I used quotation marks?
Have I started big quotations on a new line?
Have I written my quotations on lines as in the text?
Have I introduced my quotations by using a colon (:)?

Style
Is my writing too chatty?
Am I writing in an appropriate style?
Have I written in complete sentences?
Is my handwriting clear and neat?

Length
Have I written between 3 and 4 sides on A4 paper for my answer?
(If you use any pages for notes, just draw a line through them.)

- At the beginning of this test, you have **15 minutes** to read the paper and make notes but you must not start to write your answers until you are told to.

- You have **1 hour and 30 minutes** to write your answers.

- You should answer **ALL** the questions in Sections A and B.

- Then choose **ONE** question only from Section C.

- You should spend about

    15 minutes on question 1

    10 minutes on question 2

    15 minutes on question 3

    30 minutes on question 4

    5 minutes checking your work.

- Check your work carefully.

Psst!

Don't be afraid to underline, circle or highlight the key points in the texts as you are reading them. You can write in the margin, too.

Read the following passage.

Then answer question 1 and question 2.

In this story, Peter swaps bodies with the family cat and experiences what life is like from its point of view.

What a delight to walk on four soft white paws. He could see his whiskers springing out from the sides of his face, and he felt his tail curling behind him. His tread was light, and his fur was like the most comfortable of old woollen jumpers. As his pleasure in being a cat grew, his heart welled, and a tingling sensation deep in his throat became so strong that he could actually hear himself. Peter was purring. He was Peter Cat, and over there was William Boy. . .

That night Peter was too restless, too excited, too much of a cat to sleep. Towards ten o'clock he slipped through the cat flap. The freezing night air could not penetrate his thick fur coat. He padded soundlessly towards the garden wall. It towered above him, but one effortless, graceful leap and he was up, surveying his territory. How wonderful to see into dark corners, to feel every vibration of the night air on his whiskers, and to make himself invisible, when at midnight, a fox came up the garden path to root amongst the dustbins. All around he was aware of other cats, some local, some from far away, going about their night-time business, travelling their routes. After the fox, a young tabby had tried to enter the garden. Peter warned him off with a hiss and a flick of his tail. He had purred inwardly as the young fellow squealed in astonishment and took flight.

Not long after that, while patrolling the high wall that rose above the greenhouse, he came face to face with another cat, a more dangerous intruder. It was completely black, which was why Peter had not seen it sooner. It was the tom from next door, a vigorous fellow almost twice his size, with a thick neck and long powerful legs. Without even thinking, Peter arched his back and upended his fur to make himself look big.

'Hey puss,' he hissed, 'this is my wall and you're on it.'

The black cat looked surprised. It smiled. 'So it was your wall once, Grandad. What'ya going to do about it now?'

'Beat it, before I throw you off.' Peter was amazed at how strongly he felt. This was his wall, his garden, and it was his job to keep unfriendly cats out.

The black cat smiled again, coldly. 'Listen, Grandad. It hasn't been your wall for a long time. I'm coming through. Out of my way or I'll rip your fur off.'

Peter stood his ground. 'Take another step, you walking flea circus, and I'll tie your whiskers around your neck.'

The black cat gave out a long, laughing wail of contempt. But it did not take another step. All around, local cats were appearing out of the darkness to watch. Peter heard their voices.

A fight?

A fight!

The old boy must be crazy!

He's seventeen if he's a day.

The black cat arched its powerful spine and howled again, a terrible rising note.

Peter tried to keep his voice calm, but his words came out in a hiss. 'You don't take ssshort cutsss here without asking me firssst.'

The black cat blinked. The muscles in its fat neck rippled as it shrieked its laugh that was also a war cry.

On the opposite wall, a moan of excitement ran through the crowd, which was still growing.

'Old Bill has flipped.'

'He's chosen the wrong cat to pick a fight with.'

'Listen, you toothless old sheep,' the black cat said through a hiss more penetrating than Peter's. 'I'm number one round here. Isn't that right?'

The black cat half turned to the crowd, which murmured its agreement. Peter thought the watching cats did not sound very enthusiastic.

'My advice to you,' the black cat went on, 'is to step aside. Or I'll spread your guts all over the lawn.'

Peter knew he had gone too far now to back down. He extended his claws to take a firm grip on the wall. 'You bloated rat! This is my wall d'you hear . . .'

Peter had an old cat's body, but he had a young boy's mind. He ducked and felt the paw and its vicious outstretched claws go singing through the air above his ears. He had time to see how the black cat was supported momentarily on only three legs. Immediately he sprang forward, and with his two front paws pushed the tom hard in the chest. It was not the kind of thing a cat does in a fight and the number one cat was taken by surprise. With a yelp of astonishment, he slipped and tottered backwards, tipped off the wall and fell head first through the roof of the greenhouse below. The icy night air was shattered by the crash and musical tinkle of broken glass and the earthier clatter of breaking flowerpots. Then there was silence. The hushed crowd of cats peered down from their wall. They heard a movement, then a groan. Then, just visible in the gloom was the shape of the black cat hobbling across the lawn. They heard it muttering.

'It's not fair. Claws and teeth, yes. But pushing like that. It just isn't fair.'

'Next time,' Peter called down, 'you just ask permission.'

The black cat did not reply, but something about its retreating, limping shape made it clear it had understood.

The next morning Peter lay on the shelf above the radiator with his head cushioned on one paw, while the other dangled loosely in the rising warmth. All about him was hurry and chaos. Kate could not find her satchel. The porridge was burned. Mr Fortune was in a bad mood because the coffee had run out and he needed three strong cups to start the day. The kitchen was a mess and the mess was covered in porridge smoke. And it was late late late!

Peter curled his tail around his back paws and tried not to purr too loudly. On the far side of the room was his old body with William Cat inside, and that body had to go to school. William Boy was looking confused. He had his coat on and he was ready to leave but he was wearing only one shoe. The other was nowhere to be found. 'Mum,' he kept bleating. 'Where's my shoe?' But Mrs Fortune was in the hallway arguing with someone on the phone.

Peter Cat half closed his eyes. After his victory he was desperately tired. Soon the family would be gone. The house would fall silent. When the radiator had cooled, he would wander upstairs and find the most comfortable of the beds. For old time's sake he would choose his own.

The day passed just as he had hoped. Dozing, lapping a saucer of milk, dozing again, munching through some tinned cat food that really was not as bad as it smelled – rather like shepherd's pie without mashed potato. Then more dozing. Before he knew it, the sky outside was darkening and the children were home from school. William Boy looked worn out from a day of classroom and playground struggle. Boy-cat and cat-boy lay down together in front of the living-room fire. It was most odd, Peter Cat thought, to be stroked by a hand that only the day before had belonged to him.

Ian McEwan – The Daydreamer

Question 1

Write about how the writer (Ian McEwan) successfully creates the world of the cat for the reader.

In your answer you should concentrate on:

- What the character does and how he acts in his new life.
- How he writes about the senses: what the character feels, sees, hears, etc.
- The reactions of the character in his new role.
- The way he describes these and his use of language.

Refer to words or phrases in the passage to support your ideas.

10

Question 2

Explain how the cat solves the problem of the fight and why this was not seen as appropriate by the other animal.

In your answer you should comment on:

- What the problem is and how it emerges.
- How the characters deal with the confrontation in the early stages.
- The reactions of the other animals – and what they expect.
- How the boy deals with the fight.

Refer to words or phrases in the passage to support your ideas.

Use pages 7 and 8 for your notes.

8

TOTAL

18

He seems to be more impressed and excited.
delighted to walk on soft paws.
Warm

1. The writer successfully creates the world of the cat straight from the first sentence, where it describes how he is delighted to 'walk on soft paws'. The cat is very excited at what adventures he would be able to get up too and he laughs at his old body. He became stronger by the minute as he had a 'tingling sensation' and he can't seem to wait to get outside. He is more courageous in his new body and he is more braver than he would have been in his old body during the fight. The cat sees the world ahead of him waiting for him to jump out and succeed in whatever he is doing. It feels strange for the cat at first because of the tail and the whiskers but he still grew confident. He feels very warm in his 'thick fur coat' and in the freezing cold air. He ~~ignores everyone~~ becomes very brave and becomes the boss after he scares a fox and he took flight. He is very happy in his new world 'as it was wonderful to see into dark corners and to feel every vibration of the night air on his whiskers.' The human matters mean nothing to him anymore as he 'gracefully'

Jumps up the wall in one effort. This makes us feel[s]how we do about cats as we see them wondering about on the streets.

The cat talks to the other cat in a very strong and fierce way by hissing 'hey puss'. He is trying to make his feelings heard b[y]to his rival by saying 'and you're on it. He starts to get angry, once he has been called 'grandad' and when he has been asked what ya going to do.'

Read the pages from this leaflet issued by the RSPCA.

Then answer question 3.

From *Cats and Kittens*, RSPCA Animal Care

New house
If moving house seems traumatic to you, imagine what it feels like for your cat. Your new home will seem very foreign and your cat's instinct may well be to leave to find a place that feels like home.

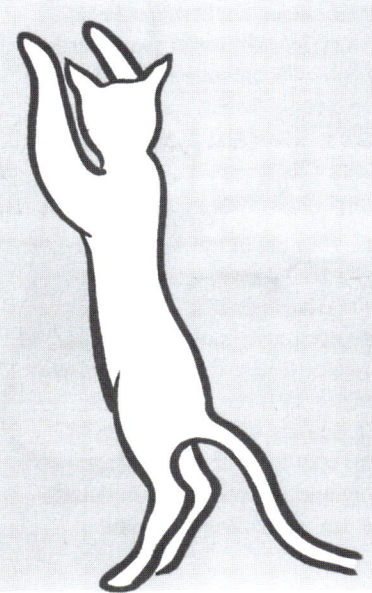

To stop this happening

1. Don't let your cat out of the basket until you've got one room straight, along with familiar objects where you can safely put it.

2. Close the windows and doors before you release your cat. Give it a meal, a litter tray and then let it roam about the room to get acclimatised. Make a big fuss of your cat - this is very reassuring.

3. Leave your cat inside overnight. If the house is fairly quiet let it explore the rest of the place as long as the doors and windows are closed. Don't let it outside yet.

4. When you feel your cat has settled - this could take two days or even a week - you can slowly start introducing it to the outside world. Do this by preparing your cat's food at its usual meal time and make sure it knows what you are doing. Don't feed it right away but encourage it to follow you outside for a short walk. The minute you get back in give it some food. If you are worried that your cat may run away if you take it into the garden, you could put it on a lead (proper harness) first before you take it for a stroll.

5. Make sure your cat is microchipped – your vet will be able to provide details, but this is one of the best ways to prevent loss. The microchip which is no bigger than a grain of rice contains all ownership details, is linked to a central computer, and can be inserted painlessly under the skin. Local authorities, dog wardens, veterinary surgeons and RSPCA animal centres all hold scanners which can be passed over lost animals revealing ownership and even medical details in seconds.

You may also, for the first week or so, like your cat to wear a collar giving your name, new address and phone number. Any collar used should be made either wholly or partly of elastic 2.5 to 4 cm (1-1.5 in) wide that will stretch enough for the cat to slip its head through if it ever becomes caught up on a branch or railing. But sadly, even the elastic precaution may not be enough - a cat caught in a tree by its own collar may struggle until the collar twists into a figure eight shape, becomes a noose and strangles it.

Settling down

Some cats adjust very quickly to a new home, while others may take up to three weeks to settle down. The important thing to remember is that cats are most likely to get lost or will make an effort to get back to their old home if they've been frightened and are in a panic. As long as they're given time to get their bearings all should be well.

Question 3

This RSPCA leaflet is given to people who become owners of a cat from a Rescue Centre.

TOTAL

10

How effective do you think the pages from this booklet are in getting the message of the RSPCA across simply and clearly?

In your answer you should comment on:

- The language which is used to suit the reader.

- The way language is used to inform and influence the reader.

- The layout of the leaflet.

- The way it makes an emotional appeal.

Refer to words and phrases in the leaflet to support your ideas.

Use this page and page 12 for your notes.

_____

_____

_____

_____

_____

_____

_____

_____

_____

_____

_____

_____

_____

_____

_____

_____

This section of the paper is a test of writing. You will be assessed on:

Your ideas and the way you organise them;

Your ability to write clearly, using paragraphs and accurate grammar, spelling and punctuation.

Question 4 Choose ONE of the following:

EITHER

a   Imagine you were able to live for a day inside the body of an animal of your choice. Describe what life would be like.

In your answer you should:

- Choose any animal you think appropriate.
- Consider what the rest of the world appears like from its point of view – shape, size, etc.
- Write about some of the situations which occur and how you react to them.

OR

b   Write about a threatening situation – for example a fight.

In your answer you could:

- Write about a real or a made-up event.
- Try to create the atmosphere of place in your description.
- Think about how you could build up tension and suspense.

OR

c   Imagine you have been asked to give a talk to a class of primary school children about the important aspects to think about before deciding to keep a pet. Write your speech.

In your answer you should:

- Write in an appropriate style for a speech.
- Make it clear you know how much your audience can understand.
- Use examples to illustrate your points.

Use page 14 for your notes.

TOTAL

32

13

General points – notes for parents

It is difficult to mark answers in an English test because there is often not a 'right answer' as there could be in Maths. The questions are often open to interpretation. Examiners for the English paper do not have a rigid mark scheme, but they will have a number of important points which will need to be covered to achieve a particular score. The more difficult the point, the more marks. There is not an expectation that a candidate will find all the points. Marking is focused on the impression created by the answer.

A mark scheme is provided for each question. You will need to judge how well the points made in the answer match with the score criteria. Any point should be clearly stated – you should not have to dig beneath the surface to find the relevant point. The most effective way of assessing work at home is to mark the piece with your child so you both can see how the final score is calculated. This will involve discussion of what is in the answer and what has been omitted and so can form a learning experience in itself.

It is also helpful for you, do the test yourself before marking it.

SECTION A

Question 1   10 marks in total

Write about how the writer (Ian McEwan) successfully creates the world of the cat for the reader.

In your answer you should concentrate on:

● What the character does and how he acts in his new life.

● How he writes about the senses: what the character feels, sees, hears, etc.

● The reactions of the character in his new role.

● The way he describes these and his use of language.

Key points

● The opening paragraph immediately gives us a feeling of what it might be like to be a cat. The writer appeals to the senses – 'walk . . . soft white paws'. He realises the animal walks in a different way. He shows that whiskers and tail are large and important physical feature to cats. He describes his light tread. The purr emerges from him as a sense of pleasure.   **2 marks**

● The writer also uses carefully chosen language to describe the features – the softness of the tread of the cat, suggesting caution; the whiskers 'springing', suggesting life; the tail 'curling', reinforcing the idea that a cat's tail is constantly moving in a smooth way; and the fur being comfortable like an 'old woollen jumper'. Cats give us the impression as they move of being completely at ease with their bodies and the environment.   **2 marks**

● Peter is now more awake at night – cats are more nocturnal – and he does not feel the cold. He moves like a cat ('padded soundlessly') and can see and feel more sensitively as a cat – 'every vibration of the night air on his whiskers'. He can jump very high up the wall and is aware of all the animal happenings in the environment – the human aspects of the world no longer matter to him. When he first meets the black cat he is surprised by his instinct to protect his territory and by his aggression towards the animal. He has no previous knowledge of how animals behave in this environment. When he communicates his 'words [come] out in a hiss' suggesting the cat's aggression. He 'arched his back and upended his fur' – an instinctive reaction in a cat to 'make himself look big'. **4 marks**

- Later, following his cat-like characteristics, he picks the warmest spot to lie – the radiator shelf – and plans to move to the warmth of the bed later. He describes a typical cat-like pose – the paw dangling, the 'head cushioned in one paw'. He describes the day in the life of a cat – 'dozing, lapping a saucer of milk, dozing again' and ends the extract in front of the fire being stroked. **2 marks**

Score	Criterion	National Curriculum Level
9 or 10	Exceptional answer	Level 7+
7 or 8	Well above average answer	Level 7
5 or 6	Above average answer	Level 6
3 or 4	Average or below average answer	Level 5
1 or 2	Well below average answer	Level 4 or below

Question 2 — 8 marks in total

Explain how the cat solves the problem of the fight and why this was not seen as appropriate by the other animal.

In your answer you should comment on:

- What the problem is and how it emerges.
- How the characters deal with the confrontation in the early stages.
- The reactions of the other animals – and what they expect.
- How the boy deals with the fight.

Key points

- The problem emerges because the boy 'inside' the cat is not aware of the way animals are expected to react in their environment. He still thinks as a human. **2 marks**

- Presumably the cat which Peter has 'taken over' is an old cat – 'He's seventeen if he's a day' – hence the 'Grandad' references. He would normally give way to the younger black cat. They both challenge each other but the black cat is confident – and would rightly be so if he were fighting a 'normal' cat. Compared to Peter he is 'twice his size' and much stronger. **2 marks**

- The animals think the situation is amusing and the black cat stays to enjoy the fight. He does give Peter the opportunity to back down. The other cats stand around and watch – expecting Peter to be defeated. **2 marks**

- When the black cat strikes, Peter uses his human reasoning to assess the situation. The cat will be balanced on three legs at a certain time and hence he could be attacked with surprise. The black cat has strength and youth to fight with. Peter is able to launch himself and push the cat from the wall by catching him off-balance. He behaves in an 'un-cat-like' way and this ensures him success. This is seen as unfair tactics by the other cats. **2 marks**

Score	Criterion	National Curriculum Level
8	Exceptional answer	Level 7+
6 or 7	Well above average answer	Level 7
5	Above average answer	Level 6
3 or 4	Average or below average answer	Level 5
1 or 2	Well below average answer	Level 4 or below

SECTION B

Question 3   **10 marks in total**

This RSPCA leaflet is given to people who become owners of a cat from a Rescue Centre.

How effective do you think the pages from this leaflet are in getting the message of the RSPCA across simply and clearly?

In your answer you should comment on:

- The language which is used to suit the reader.

- The way language is used to inform and influence the reader.

- The layout of the leaflet.

- The way it makes an emotional appeal.

Key points

- The leaflet aims to present information as simply and effectively as possible. The information which it is giving is practical and based on experience. The audience will be one that knows the language and subject matter – will be cat-lovers – as they have bothered to go to a cat rescue centre to find a new pet.
  2 marks

- The language used is direct and uses the second person 'You' to talk to the audience. It is almost like having a conversation. Straight away, it puts the situation into a personal context by making the reader imagine what the situation of moving house would be like for him/her. Then they can 'imagine what it feels like for your cat.' The solutions to the problem are given succinctly in number form. The instructions use the imperative (command) tone – 'Close … Leave … Make sure …'. These are very practical – even down to warning owners about the dangers of collars.
  3 marks

- The passage is about moving into a new house with a cat and the design reflects this with the house shapes on the page. These also serve to separate out parts of the text in order to make them easier to read. The final 'box' contains the conclusion which reassures the reader and cat owner if something should go wrong, e.g. their cat should wander off. All through the leaflet, sub-headings are used so that the reader can judge which part of the text is more relevant to him or her. In all it is about clarity, using simple language and a personal response to the reader.
  3 marks

- The leaflet provides a mix of graphics and text to make its impact – emotional and factual. The photographs of cats are very appealing. One shows a cat behind bars which appeals to our sympathies; the other shows a contented cat in a home/garden situation. Cartoons are used to create a more amusing, playful effect.
  2 marks

Score	Criterion	National Curriculum Level
9 or 10	Exceptional answer	Level 7+
7 or 8	Well above average answer	Level 7
5 or 6	Above average answer	Level 6
3 or 4	Average or below average answer	Level 5
1 or 2	Well below average answer	Level 4 or below

SECTION C

Question 4 (writing test)

This question is marked for overall impression – there is not a set of correct points which should be incorporated. Both content and how the content is communicated – style, grammar, punctuation, accuracy – are all considered.

However there is a set of marking criteria which need to be considered:

Does the answer:	Yes	No
Communicate ideas clearly to you?		
Use a suitable style for the purpose indicated in the question?		
Organise the material in an appropriate way to the style?		
Use paragraphs, correct grammar and punctuation?		
Spell words correctly and make use of relevant words precisely?		
Look neat and make reading easy?		

On the next page is a guide to the National Curriculum writing criteria. Mark your child's work by how many of the features are included and how effectively.

Level 4	Yes	No
Ideas clearly expressed		
Paragraphs – organised ideas		
Punctuation to separate sentences generally accurate		
Spelling of simple words accurate		
Handwriting clear and legible		

Level 5	Yes	No
Ideas clearly expressed		
Wide vocabulary, precise use of words		
Simple and complex sentences used and made into paragraphs		
Variety of punctuation – apostrophes and commas used correctly		
Spelling words – complex regular patterns – accurate		
Handwriting – clear, legible, fluent		

Level 6	Yes	No
Ideas clearly expressed with a sense of purpose		
A varied vocabulary used – appropriate language expressed in simple and complex sentences – good paragraphing		
Spelling accurate – some difficult words still incorrect		
Range of punctuation used – some more difficult forms		
Handwriting fluent and legible		

Level 7	Yes	No
Confidently expressed ideas – words chosen are appropriate		
Appropriate style is matched by appropriate language		
Accurate grammar and punctuation consciously used for effect		
Correct paragraphing and punctuation		
Spelling of irregular words correct		
Handwriting consistently fluent and legible		

If your child needs more practice in any English topic, he or she could use the WHSmith Key Stage 3 English Revision Guide.

Preparing for the Shakespeare paper

There's only one way to prepare for answering questions on a Shakespeare play – read the play! Watching the video is not good enough.

In your test, you will be asked to deal with one aspect of the play you have studied in relation to one or two scenes, but you must also be prepared to share your knowledge of the rest of the play by putting certain aspects of the play into context and say what has happened before – and if anything has changed – and even what will happen later in the play.

The questions in this book give you a flavour of the kinds of questions you could find in your final tests. Even if the question in front of you on the day looks different from any question you have dealt with in school, don't panic! You will have the information you need if you stop to think.

You will not be allowed to take the text into the test; you need to rely on your memory and understanding of the work you have done in Year 9.

Remember: Do not write everything you know about the play – you are not being tested on how good your memory is. Answer the question you have been set – not the one you want to be set!

Handy hints for answering the questions

Draft your answer before you finally write it:

- Take time to think about what information you need from the scene printed for you.

- Spend at least 15 minutes carefully reading the scene you have chosen.

- Do not be afraid to underline or circle important quotations. Write notes in the margin as you go along.

- Use the helpful pointers given to you on the question paper and write notes on each section. Prove each of your points with a brief quotation.

- Do not write out huge sections from the play. The examiner wants to know what and how **you** write – not how Shakespeare did!

It is important that you time yourself effectively. You need to pace yourself. You have time to read and annotate the scene printed for you and time to draft and write your answer. You will not be given extra time.

You are being assessed in this section on your knowledge and awareness of the Shakespeare play you have studied – its plot, ideas, the characters and why they behave in the way they do, the language and even the staging of the scene. But remember, you will also have to write clearly to communicate these ideas. Hence marks are allocated for use of appropriate style, clarity and for the organisation of writing, spelling, grammar and punctuation. Your handwriting is also important, so leave enough time to check your work.

Marking the tests

Your work on a Shakespeare play will be considered from two points of view:

- **Understanding and response:** the content of what you write – how you have understood and responded to Shakespeare and his ideas, how his characters behave and why they do, the development and changes in the plot and his language.

- **Written expression:** the way you write – your choice of appropriate style, your use of paragraphs, vocabulary, punctuation and spelling as well as your ability to write clearly and legibly.

There is not a 'perfect answer': everyone's response will be different

To achieve the highest grades you will need to:

- Know and understand your Shakespeare play well

- Write clearly and to the point – do not ramble on, giving irrelevant information from the play just because you know it

- Answer the question you have been set in an organised way

- Write from a personal point of view so the examiner gets a sense of what you think and feel – not just what your teacher said

- Write accurately in clear, well-punctuated English, using well-constructed sentences.

If you have studied *Henry V* do this task.

75 minutes are allowed

Your work will be assessed for your knowledge and understanding of the play and the way you express your ideas.

Check your work carefully.

Henry V

Act 2 Scene 2

- Before the King departs to the wars in France, he reveals Scroop, Cambridge and Grey as traitors.
- Imagine you are going to direct this scene for a class performance.
- Explain how you will want the pupil acting the part of Henry V to show how he is a King to be reckoned with and that he has changed from the reckless prince that he was once thought.

Before you write you should decide what advice to give the pupil about:

- What the assembled Lords used to think about the King and how an earlier scene with the French envoy had changed this
- How the King should behave to the traitors in the early part of the scene
- How the King allows them to give their own views on punishment and mercy and how he cleverly judges them by this later
- How the King shows them he knows about their intended crimes and what this shows about his character
- How the King's tone changes when their crimes are revealed and how the actor must use Henry V's language to show his thoughts and feelings in the scene
- How the final part of the scene gives the audience an indication of how the King will behave in France

Read the task again before you begin to write your answer.

> **EXAMINER'S TIP**
> Remind yourself about some of the following points:
> - Set the scene in the context of the rest of the play. Henry was once seen as a 'tearaway' ('His hours filled up with riots, banquets, sports') but when he became King he realised he would have to take on the responsibility ('The King is full of grace and fair regard'). We have already seen him deal with the French Ambassador ('Tell him he hath made a match with such a wrangler…').
> - Henry knows the men in front of him are traitors and plays along with them until they state their own punishment. This is a mature King, a clever and manipulative politician. He is 'his own man' and the passion of his words against the three traitors shows his patriotism. The final speech gives us a sense of what he will be like at Agincourt.

Act 2 Scene 2

Southampton. A council-chamber.

Trumpets sound. Enter KING HENRY V, SCROOP, CAMBRIDGE, GREY, and Attendants

King Henry V	Now sits the wind fair, and we will aboard. My Lord of Cambridge, and my kind Lord of Masham, And you, my gentle knight, give me your thoughts: Think you not that the powers we bear with us Will cut their passage through the force of France, Doing the execution and the act For which we have in head assembled them?
Scroop	No doubt, my liege, if each man do his best.
King Henry V	I doubt not that; since we are well persuaded We carry not a heart with us from hence That grows not in a fair consent with ours, Nor leave not one behind that doth not wish Success and conquest to attend on us.
Cambridge	Never was monarch better fear'd and loved Than is your majesty: there's not, I think, a subject That sits in heart-grief and uneasiness Under the sweet shade of your government.
Grey	True: those that were your father's enemies Have steep'd their galls in honey and do serve you With hearts create of duty and of zeal.
King Henry V	We therefore have great cause of thankfulness; And shall forget the office of our hand, Sooner than quittance of desert and merit According to the weight and worthiness.
Scroop	So service shall with steeled sinews toil, And labour shall refresh itself with hope, To do your grace incessant services.
King Henry V	We judge no less. Uncle of Exeter, Enlarge the man committed yesterday, That rail'd against our person: we consider It was excess of wine that set him on; And on his more advice we pardon him.
Scroop	That's mercy, but too much security: Let him be punish'd, sovereign, lest example Breed, by his sufferance, more of such a kind.

King Henry V	O, let us yet be merciful.
Cambridge	So may your highness, and yet punish too.
Grey	Sir, You show great mercy, if you give him life, After the taste of much correction.
King Henry V	Alas, your too much love and care of me Are heavy orisons 'gainst this poor wretch! If little faults, proceeding on distemper, Shall not be wink'd at, how shall we stretch our eye When capital crimes, chew'd, swallow'd and digested, Appear before us? We'll yet enlarge that man, Though Cambridge, Scroop and Grey, in their dear care And tender preservation of our person, Would have him punished. And now to our French causes: Who are the late commissioners?
Cambridge	I one, my lord: Your highness bade me ask for it to-day.
Scroop	So did you me, my liege.
Grey	And I, my royal sovereign.
King Henry V	Then, Richard Earl of Cambridge, there is yours; There yours, Lord Scroop of Masham; and, sir knight, Grey of Northumberland, this same is yours: Read them; and know, I know your worthiness. My Lord of Westmoreland, and uncle Exeter, We will aboard to night. Why, how now, gentlemen! What see you in those papers that you lose So much complexion? Look ye, how they change! Their cheeks are paper. Why, what read you there That hath so cowarded and chased your blood Out of appearance?
Cambridge	I do confess my fault; And do submit me to your highness' mercy.
Grey; Scroop	To which we all appeal.
King Henry V	The mercy that was quick in us but late, By your own counsel is suppress'd and kill'd: You must not dare, for shame, to talk of mercy; For your own reasons turn into your bosoms, As dogs upon their masters, worrying you.

See you, my princes, and my noble peers,
These English monsters! My Lord of Cambridge here,
You know how apt our love was to accord
To furnish him with all appertinents
Belonging to his honour; and this man
Hath, for a few light crowns, lightly conspired,
And sworn unto the practices of France,
To kill us here in Hampton: to the which
This knight, no less for bounty bound to us
Than Cambridge is, hath likewise sworn. But, O,
What shall I say to thee, Lord Scroop? thou cruel,
Ingrateful, savage and inhuman creature!
Thou that didst bear the key of all my counsels,
That knew'st the very bottom of my soul,
That almost mightst have coin'd me into gold,
Wouldst thou have practised on me for thy use,
May it be possible, that foreign hire
Could out of thee extract one spark of evil
That might annoy my finger? 'tis so strange,
That, though the truth of it stands off as gross
As black and white, my eye will scarcely see it.
Treason and murder ever kept together,
As two yoke-devils sworn to either's purpose,
Working so grossly in a natural cause,
That admiration did not whoop at them:
But thou, 'gainst all proportion, didst bring in
Wonder to wait on treason and on murder:
And whatsoever cunning fiend it was
That wrought upon thee so preposterously
Hath got the voice in hell for excellence:
All other devils that suggest by treasons
Do botch and bungle up damnation
With patches, colours, and with forms being fetch'd
From glistering semblances of piety;
But he that temper'd thee bade thee stand up,
Gave thee no instance why thou shouldst do treason,
Unless to dub thee with the name of traitor.
If that same demon that hath gull'd thee thus
Should with his lion gait walk the whole world,
He might return to vasty Tartar back,
And tell the legions 'I can never win
A soul so easy as that Englishman's.'
O, how hast thou with jealousy infected
The sweetness of affiance! Show men dutiful?
Why, so didst thou: seem they grave and learned?
Why, so didst thou: come they of noble family?
Why, so didst thou: seem they religious?
Why, so didst thou: or are they spare in diet,

Free from gross passion or of mirth or anger,
Constant in spirit, not swerving with the blood,
Garnish'd and deck'd in modest complement,
Not working with the eye without the ear,
And but in purged judgment trusting neither?
Such and so finely bolted didst thou seem:
And thus thy fall hath left a kind of blot,
To mark the full-fraught man and best indued
With some suspicion. I will weep for thee;
For this revolt of thine, methinks, is like
Another fall of man. Their faults are open:
Arrest them to the answer of the law;
And God acquit them of their practices!

Exeter

I arrest thee of high treason, by the name of
Richard Earl of Cambridge.
I arrest thee of high treason, by the name of
Henry Lord Scroop of Masham.
I arrest thee of high treason, by the name of
Thomas Grey, knight, of Northumberland.

Scroop

Our purposes God justly hath discover'd;
And I repent my fault more than my death;
Which I beseech your highness to forgive,
Although my body pay the price of it.

Cambridge

For me, the gold of France did not seduce;
Although I did admit it as a motive
The sooner to effect what I intended:
But God be thanked for prevention;
Which I in sufferance heartily will rejoice,
Beseeching God and you to pardon me.

Grey

Never did faithful subject more rejoice
At the discovery of most dangerous treason
Than I do at this hour joy o'er myself.
Prevented from a damned enterprise:
My fault, but not my body, pardon, sovereign.

King Henry V

God quit you in his mercy! Hear your sentence.
You have conspired against our royal person,
Join'd with an enemy proclaim'd and from his coffers
Received the golden earnest of our death;
Wherein you would have sold your king to slaughter,
His princes and his peers to servitude,
His subjects to oppression and contempt
And his whole kingdom into desolation.
Touching our person seek we no revenge;

But we our kingdom's safety must so tender,
Whose ruin you have sought, that to her laws
We do deliver you. Get you therefore hence,
Poor miserable wretches, to your death:
The taste whereof, God of his mercy give
You patience to endure, and true repentance
Of all your dear offences! Bear them hence.

Exeunt CAMBRIDGE, SCROOP and GREY, guarded

Now, lords, for France; the enterprise whereof
Shall be to you, as us, like glorious.
We doubt not of a fair and lucky war,
Since God so graciously hath brought to light
This dangerous treason lurking in our way
To hinder our beginnings. We doubt not now
But every rub is smoothed on our way.
Then forth, dear countrymen: let us deliver
Our puissance into the hand of God,
Putting it straight in expedition.
Cheerly to sea; the signs of war advance:
No king of England, if not king of France.

Exeunt

If you have studied *Twelfth Night* do this task.

75 minutes are allowed

Your work will be assessed for your knowledge and understanding of the play and the way you express your ideas.

Check your work carefully.

Twelfth Night

Act 3 Scene 4

● This play is referred to as a 'comedy' although some aspects are more serious. Explain how Shakespeare makes us laugh in this scene, but how later we may find Malvolio's humiliation less amusing.

Before you begin to write you should think about:

● What we have learned about Malvolio before and what we feel about him.

● Why the others have decided to play this trick on him.

● How the trick works and the way Malvolio reacts.

● What happens as a result of the trick and what it shows about his character.

● How the trick is discovered and what happens.

● How we feel about the trick at the end of the play.

Read the task again before you begin to write your answer.

EXAMINER'S TIP

Remind yourself about some of the following points:

● Set the scene in the context of the rest of the play. We have already seen Malvolio as a vain, selfish person ('You are sick of self-love Malvolio...') who does not like to see the others having fun ('Dos't thou think, because thou art virtuous, there shall be no more cakes and ale?').

● Finding the letter appeals to his sense of pride. He really believes he is important enough to be loved by Olivia, even though there is no proof at all. The others try to make Olivia think he is mad 'possessed'.

● Malvolio appears cross-gartered in front of Olivia completely out of character and acts in an outrageous way – 'he does nothing but smile'. Olivia hates the fashion. She cannot understand why he is acting in this way. He continually quotes the letter he has found – 'Be not afraid of greatness'. We know that he will follow the words of the letter and treat Sir Toby with contempt.

● The scene is amusing in its mistaken identities, its language and its staging.

Act 3 Scene 4

OLIVIA's garden.

Enter OLIVIA and MARIA

Olivia	I have sent after him: he says he'll come; How shall I feast him? what bestow of him? For youth is bought more oft than begg'd or borrow'd. I speak too loud. Where is Malvolio? he is sad and civil, And suits well for a servant with my fortunes: Where is Malvolio?
Maria	He's coming, madam; but in very strange manner. He is, sure, possessed, madam.
Olivia	Why, what's the matter? does he rave?
Maria	No, madam, he does nothing but smile: your ladyship were best to have some guard about you, if he come; for, sure, the man is tainted in's wits.
Olivia	Go call him hither.

Exit MARIA

	I am as mad as he, If sad and merry madness equal be.

Re-enter MARIA, with MALVOLIO

	How now, Malvolio!
Malvolio	Sweet lady, ho, ho.
Olivia	Smilest thou? I sent for thee upon a sad occasion.
Malvolio	Sad, lady! I could be sad: this does make some obstruction in the blood, this cross-gartering; but what of that? if it please the eye of one, it is with me as the very true sonnet is, 'Please one, and please all.'
Olivia	Why, how dost thou, man? what is the matter with thee?
Malvolio	Not black in my mind, though yellow in my legs. It did come to his hands, and commands shall be executed: I think we do know the sweet Roman hand.
Olivia	Wilt thou go to bed, Malvolio?

Malvolio	To bed! ay, sweet-heart, and I'll come to thee.
Olivia	God comfort thee! Why dost thou smile so and kiss thy hand so oft?
Maria	How do you, Malvolio?
Malvolio	At your request! yes; nightingales answer daws.
Maria	Why appear you with this ridiculous boldness before my lady?
Malvolio	'Be not afraid of greatness:' 'twas well writ.
Olivia	What meanest thou by that, Malvolio?
Malvolio	'Some are born great,'—
Olivia	Ha!
Malvolio	'Some achieve greatness,'—
Olivia	What sayest thou?
Malvolio	'And some have greatness thrust upon them.'
Olivia	Heaven restore thee!
Malvolio	'Remember who commended thy yellow stockings,'—
Olivia	Thy yellow stockings!
Malvolio	'And wished to see thee cross-gartered.'
Olivia	Cross-gartered!
Malvolio	'Go to thou art made, if thou desirest to be so;'—
Olivia	Am I made?
Malvolio	'If not, let me see thee a servant still.'
Olivia	Why, this is very midsummer madness.

Enter SERVANT

Servant	Madam, the young gentleman of the Count Orsino's is returned: I could hardly entreat him back: he attends your ladyship's pleasure.
Olivia	I'll come to him.

Exit SERVANT

Good Maria, let this fellow be looked to. Where's my cousin Toby? Let some of my people have a special care of him: I would not have him miscarry for the half of my dowry.

Exeunt OLIVIA and MARIA

Malvolio   O, ho! do you come near me now? no worse man than Sir Toby to look to me! This concurs directly with the letter: she sends him on purpose, that I may appear stubborn to him; for she incites me to that in the letter. 'Cast thy humble slough,' says she; 'be opposite with a kinsman, surly with servants; let thy tongue tang with arguments of state; put thyself into the trick of singularity;' and consequently sets down the manner how; as, a sad face, a reverend carriage, a slow tongue, in the habit of some sir of note, and so forth. I have limed her; but it is Jove's doing, and Jove make me thankful! And when she went away now, 'Let this fellow be looked to:' fellow! not Malvolio, nor after my degree, but fellow. Why, every thing adheres together, that no dram of a scruple, no scruple of a scruple, no obstacle, no incredulous or unsafe circumstance—What can be said? Nothing that can be can come between me and the full prospect of my hopes. Well, Jove, not I, is the doer of this, and he is to be thanked.

Re-enter MARIA, with SIR TOBY BELCH and FABIAN

Sir Toby Belch   Which way is he, in the name of sanctity? If all the devils of hell be drawn in little, and Legion himself possessed him, yet I'll speak to him.

Fabian   Here he is, here he is. How is't with you, sir? how is't with you, man?

Malvolio   Go off; I discard you: let me enjoy my private: go off.

Come over it.

Macbeth

Lady Macbeth is not the aggressive dominant force that we have seen in other scenes. She is very worried, while waiting for her husband. She is so nervous that, she has even had a drink, "That which hath made them drunk hath made me bold" which clearly indicates that she has no confidence in her husband. She thinks that Macbeth has not dared to go through the crime, "I laid their daggers ready, He could not miss 'em" and feels that he is going to be caught red handed. This scene is full of questions e.g. "Didst thou not hear a noise?", "Did not you speak?" This clearly shows that Lady Macbeth and her husband are very scared and suspicious. They are both nervous, "Did not you speak", "When"?, "Now" as you can see Macbeth clearly did speak.

In the earlier scene (Act 2 sc 1, The dagger scene) Macbeth seemed scared as he saw the blood stained dagger hover in front of him, "Come let me clutch thee" leading him to murder Duncan. Macbeth has had serious doubts about the plot. There are two things he is scared of, the consequences and his guilty conscience. He is only doing this because his wife is "ambitious" and wants him to become king. After Lady Macbeth receives the letter from her husband she is excited. She hears better news "That croaks the fatal entrance of Duncan under my battlement", shows that she is plotting the murder.

We have seen Lady Macbeth been the dominent force but both characters seem to have panicked in this scene. They both seem to hear noises, "Didst thou not hear a noise?", which is a sigh sign of panic. They both are afraid that they will be found out. In Act 1 Scene 2, we see the "brave" soldier Macbeth in action but in the this scene we see a very different Macbeth. In my opinion he has changed because of the force of his wife. In this Scene we see Macbeth shouting "who's there? what ho!" but Lady Macbeth manages to control him again.

Shakespeare had many restrictions in them days but he still managed to create a appropiate atmosphere. He wasn't able to use lighting and all this modern day equipment but he still found his ways. He created dramatic tension in this scene by doing it in the dark. After all, dark symbolises evil and, so the atmosphere is very tense. Early in Act 2 Scene & He created tension by words and images while the audience knows it is dark as there is a owl.

Macbeth has brought back with him the bloodstained daggers. His wife is shocked that he has brought evidence with him, "why did you bring these daggers from the place", and again she controls Macbeth.

If you have studied *Macbeth* do this task.

Time allowed: 75 minutes

Your work will be assessed for your knowledge and understanding of the play and the way you express your ideas.

Check your work carefully.

Macbeth

Act 2 Scene 2

Task

This scene is the key moment of the play – the murder of Duncan.

 Show how Shakespeare builds up an atmosphere of dramatic tension on stage and between the characters.

Before you begin to write you should think about:

- How the characters act and feel during the various stages of this scene – Lady Macbeth when she is waiting for her husband; Macbeth when he returns from the murder scene.

- What the characters had felt like in the build up to the murder – what was Macbeth thinking and feeling? How did Lady Macbeth react to the idea of the murder?

- How and why the characters we have seen previously change in this scene.

- The restrictions of Shakespeare's theatre compared to today and how he managed to create the appropriate atmosphere and tension for the audience.

Read the task again before you begin to write your answer.

EXAMINER'S TIP

Remind yourself about some of the following points:

- Set the scene in the context of the rest of the play. Macbeth has been given prophecies by the three witches; one of the prophecies is that he will become king. He thinks this is impossible but, after he becomes Thane of Glamis and Cawdor, the idea of what he could do to make himself King gradually comes into his mind.

- His wife is ambitious for her husband and is aware of his character weaknesses – he is 'too full of the milk of human kindness' even though he is 'brave Macbeth' the warrior. She will have to push him into performing the act.

- Fate seems to be pushing Macbeth to murder the king, when Duncan decides to stay at Glamis castle. Lady Macbeth swears that the King 'never shall that morrow see' if he stays.

- Macbeth has had strong doubts – he is afraid of consequences and his conscience – 'If we fail?'. He has even hallucinated the 'dagger which I see before me' leading him to the murder.

- In this scene the 'brave' Macbeth seems to crumble under pressure, although both characters are very afraid and seem to imagine noises and people discovering their evil act. Lady Macbeth takes control and seems the dominant character.

- It is night, the atmosphere is tense and reflects their guilty conscience. The scene is 'full' of blood.

- The murder is discovered and Macbeth manipulates himself into the position of king but he is never happy again and 'blood will have blood they say' – this evil act leads him to many more.

Act 2 Scene II The same

[Enter LADY MACBETH]

Lady Macbeth	That which hath made them drunk hath made me bold;
	What hath quench'd them hath given me fire. Hark! Peace!
	It was the owl that shriek'd, the fatal bellman,
	Which gives the stern'st good-night. He is about it:
	The doors are open; and the surfeited grooms
	Do mock their charge with snores: I have drugg'd their possets,
	That death and nature do contend about them,
	Whether they live or die.

Macbeth [Within]	Who's there? what, ho!

Lady Macbeth	Alack, I am afraid they have awaked,
	And 'tis not done. The attempt and not the deed
	Confounds us. Hark! I laid their daggers ready;
	He could not miss 'em. Had he not resembled
	My father as he slept, I had done't.

[Enter MACBETH carrying two bloodstained daggers]

My husband!

Macbeth	I have done the deed. Didst thou not hear a noise?

Lady Macbeth	I heard the owl scream and the crickets cry.
	Did not you speak?

Macbeth	When?

Lady Macbeth	Now.

Macbeth	As I descended?

Lady Macbeth	Ay.

Macbeth	Hark!
	Who lies i' the second chamber?

Lady Macbeth	Donalbain.
Macbeth	This is a sorry sight.

[Looking on his hands]

Lady Macbeth	A foolish thought, to say a sorry sight.
Macbeth	There's one did laugh in's sleep, and one cried 'Murder!'
	That they did wake each other: I stood and heard them:
	But they did say their prayers, and address'd them
	Again to sleep.
Lady Macbeth	There are two lodged together.
Macbeth	One cried 'God bless us!' and 'Amen' the other;
	As they had seen me with these hangman's hands.
	Listening their fear, I could not say 'Amen,'
	When they did say 'God bless us!'
Lady Macbeth	Consider it not so deeply.
Macbeth	But wherefore could not I pronounce 'Amen'?
	I had most need of blessing, and 'Amen'
	Stuck in my throat.
Lady Macbeth	These deeds must not be thought
	After these ways; so, it will make us mad.
Macbeth	Methought I heard a voice cry 'Sleep no more!
	Macbeth does murder sleep', the innocent sleep, —
	Sleep that knits up the ravell'd sleeve of care,
	The death of each day's life, sore labour's bath,
	Balm of hurt minds, great nature's second course,
	Chief nourisher in life's feast.
Lady Macbeth	What do you mean?
Macbeth	Still it cried 'Sleep no more!' to all the house:
	'Glamis hath murder'd sleep, and therefore Cawdor
	Shall sleep no more; Macbeth shall sleep no more.'

Lady Macbeth   Who was it that thus cried? Why, worthy thane,
                You do unbend your noble strength, to think
                So brainsickly of things. Go get some water,
                And wash this filthy witness from your hand.
                Why did you bring these daggers from the place?
                They must lie there: go carry them; and smear
                The sleepy grooms with blood.

Macbeth   I'll go no more:
                I am afraid to think what I have done;
                Look on't again I dare not.

Lady Macbeth   Infirm of purpose!
                Give me the daggers: the sleeping and the dead
                Are but as pictures: 'tis the eye of childhood
                That fears a painted devil. If he do bleed,
                I'll gild the faces of the grooms withal;
                For it must seem their guilt.

[Exit. Knocking within]

Macbeth   Whence is that knocking?
                How is't with me, when every noise appals me?
                What hands are here? Ha! they pluck out mine eyes.
                Will all great Neptune's ocean wash this blood
                Clean from my hand? No, this my hand will rather
                The multitudinous seas in incarnadine,
                Making the green one red.

[Re-enter LADY MACBETH]

Lady Macbeth   My hands are of your colour; but I shame
                To wear a heart so white.

[Knocking within]

                I hear a knocking
                At the south entry: retire we to our chamber;
                A little water clears us of this deed:
                How easy is it, then! Your constancy
                Hath left you unattended.

[Knocking within]

Hark! more knocking.
Get on your nightgown, lest occasion call us,
And show us to be watchers. Be not lost
So poorly in your thoughts.

Macbeth   To know my deed, 'twere best not know myself.

[Knocking within]

Wake Duncan with thy knocking! I would thou couldst!

[Exeunt]

Macbeth has had three prophecies from the three witches after the battle. One was to become king. Macbeth had never thought about this untill his wife pushes him into killing ~~Ducan~~ Duncan because of her ambitions for him. She is anxiously waiting for her brave husband to return from the killing of Duncan. She is nervous but she has done everything to plan. 'That which hath made them drunk hath made me bold' means she has been drinking to calm her nerves. She has drugged their possests and laid their daggers ready.

Macbeth is sorry he has done this and he is ready to give the secret away but his wife realises that he is weak and she manages to control him. She tells him 'Go get some water and wash this filthy witness from your hand. Macbeth wants to go no further in this bloody business but his wife takes control.

Shakespeare builds up the dramatic tension in this scene by doing it while in darkness. We know that darkness symbolises evil.

Macbeth shouts out 'Who's there? What ho.' Macbeth is very scared. His wife is waiting nervously for her husband to return and here is shouting. 'Alack I am afraid they have awaked' she worries. She thinks that Macbeth has damaged the plan and he has not gone ahead with it.

After Macbeth saw the witches along with Banquo, he was feeling frightened at what these three evil women were telling him. Why were they telling this to him and not his friend. Of course Macbeth would be happy at the thought

Henry V

This paper is marked for:

- **Understanding and Response.** What is written. This tests the student's understanding of *Henry V*, its characters, themes and story as well as the language.

- **Written Expression.** How it is written. This tests the student's ability to write clear answers about the play in clear, logical, grammatically correct English.

According to the official mark scheme there are 40 marks available for the Shakespeare section of the test.

- **Understanding and Response will be marked out of 24**

21-24 marks	Exceptional performance	Above Level 7
17-20 marks	Well above average	Level 7
13-16 marks	Above average	Level 6
9-12 marks	Average/below average	Level 5
4-8 marks	Well below average	Level 4 and below

- **Written Expression will be marked out of 16. See page 44 for details of this.**

Henry V

Act 4 Scene 3

- Before the King departs to the wars in France, he reveals Scroop, Cambridge and Grey as traitors.

- Imagine you are going to direct this scene for a class performance.

- Explain how you will want the pupil acting the part of Henry V to show how he is a King to be reckoned with and that he has changed from the reckless prince that he was once thought.

Key points

Look for at least 6 of these and mark each out of 4.

- The scene marks the public awareness of the authority of the King. Previously he had been thought of as Prince Hal – the young prince who spent a dissolute life in the taverns with his friends including Falstaff, Pistol and Nym.

- Previously the French ambassador had arrived and had insulted him with the gift of tennis balls, to indicate that they thought he was still 'playful' and not to be treated seriously. However his response to them proved to the Lords present that he was serious about his country and was prepared to fight France.

- At the beginning of this scene we are aware that the King knows what the traitors have done: 'The King hath note of all that they intend', so he is cleverly playing a part with them in order that they should punish themselves.

- Henry is more than polite to them at the start: 'my kind lord … gentle night' which becomes ironic in the light of the fact that they are planning to kill Henry. He prompts them to make patriotic statements: 'Never was monarch better fear'd and loved' showing them to be hypocrites.

- He presents the traitors with a real case in law. The King is prepared to release the man who was arrested: 'we pardon him'. The traitors make a case for not showing mercy, 'lest example/Breed, by his sufferance'. They fall into Henry's trap and he cunningly and cleverly lets them. Note his continued pleasant yet bitter comments: 'in their dear care … tender preservation of our person… I know your worthiness.' This is the King disappointed by traitors. He needs people he can trust about him.

- He hands them papers. The audience thinks they are official papers but they are a summary of their crimes: 'What see you in those papers that you lose/So much complexion?' He is in a sense torturing them and there should be a sense of enjoyment from now on.

- The Lords beg for forgiveness – they ask for mercy in a way they have just denied for others. Henry's large speech is passionate and patriotic, showing his disgust of the traitors and his disappointment in them. He takes them one at a time and slowly lists their faults – 'thou cruel/Ingrateful, savage and inhuman creature!'– and calls them 'devils'.

- The traitors show their final respect for the King by humbly apologising: 'Beseeching God and you to pardon me'. He sentences them to death – it is necessary. He can show no mercy, judged by the traitors' own arguments.

- Like the true King that he is he switches directly to the matter in hand – the war in France. This gives some indication of how he will behave at the battle of Agincourt: caring for his men and their welfare but appealing to their patriotism in order to win the battle.

Twelfth Night

This paper is marked for:

- **Understanding and Response.** What is written. This tests the student's understanding of *Twelfth Night*, its characters, themes and story as well as its language.

- **Written Expression.** How it is written. This tests the student's ability to write clear answers about *Twelfth Night* in clear, logical, grammatically correct English.

According to the official mark scheme there are 40 marks available for the Shakespeare section of the test.

- **Understanding and Response will be marked out of 24**

21-24 marks	Exceptional performance	Above Level 7
17-20 marks	Well above average	Level 7
13-16 marks	Above average	Level 6
9-12 marks	Average/below average	Level 5
4-8 marks	Well below average	Level 4 and below

- **Written Expression will be marked out of 16. See page 44 for details of this.**

Twelfth Night

Act 3 Scene 4

- This play is referred to as a 'comedy' although some aspects are more serious. Explain how Shakespeare makes us laugh in this scene, but how later we may find Malvolio's humiliation less amusing.

Key points

Look for at least 6 of these and mark each out of 4.

- The scene marks the first stage in the humiliation of Malvolio. As with most comedy, the action can be interpreted in two ways. It is amusing to us, but humiliation is never very funny to the person concerned.

- Malvolio has already presented himself as a vain fool – 'You are sick of self-love Malvolio' – and he has stopped the others having fun at Olivia's house: '...because thou art virtuous, there shall be no more cakes and ale'. He is in love with the mistress of the house – an impossible occurrence because of the differences in their rank, but also because she has fallen in love with the 'youth'. We know the youth to be Viola.

- Maria plans the trick and the rest of the group hide. The audience is aware of them and can hear their comments but Malvolio cannot. When he finds the letter, he imagines that Olivia loves him: 'Maria once told me she did affect me'. He is conceited enough to believe this but is not clever enough to know that he is being tricked ('tickled'). He cannot see just how preposterous his beliefs are.

- He uses the stage and struts around imagining himself married to Olivia; he uses very affected words and phrases which he thinks those in the upper-classes would use, but in fact they would not. He imagines himself in romantic situations which contrasts to his real character: 'Calling my officers around me in my branched velvet gown'. The way he interprets the letter shows he is not so clever after all: 'If this should be thee Malvolio… M… Malvolio… why that begins my name'.

- The scene is comic as Malvolio appears cross gartered and so physically ridiculous – the style of dress is completely out of character and Olivia personally hates this style. Malvolio makes rather suggestive comments which are also out of character – 'To bed! Ay, sweet heart and I'll come to thee' – which will lead Olivia to hate him more. He smiles continually and people convince Olivia that he is mad. He quotes the letter he has found which he thinks is his key to greatness but Olivia does not understand the references and this makes his behaviour and speech – as well as his dress – seem more peculiar. He is totally humiliated and finally locked away in prison.

- His punishment does not end there because the Fool visits him disguised as a priest and taunts him. We begin to feel sorry for Malvolio at this point as the joke has gone too far but the others do not really care about this.

- The plot is revealed to Olivia and she shows pity towards him ('Alas poor fool...') but Malvolio will not be pitied. His final lines make the joke turn sour. He will not forgive them. This is not to be a 'happy ever after' play: 'I'll be revenged...' The lovers are paired off at the end but the spirit of Malvolio's last line remains.

Macbeth

This paper is marked for:

- **Understanding and Response.** What is written. This tests understanding of *Macbeth*, its characters, its themes and story as well as its language.

- **Written Expression.** How it is written. This tests the candidate's ability to write clear answers about *Macbeth* in clear, logical, grammatically correct English.

According to the official mark scheme there are 40 marks available for the Shakespeare section of the test.

- **Understanding and Response will be marked out of 24**

21-24 marks	Exceptional performance	Above Level 7
17-20 marks	Well above average	Level 7
13-16 marks	Above average	Level 6
9-12 marks	Average/below average	Level 5
4-8 marks	Well below average	Level 4 and below

- **Written Expression will be marked out of 16. See page 44 for details of this.**

Macbeth

Act 2 Scene 2

Task

This scene is the key moment of the play – the murder of Duncan.

- Show how Shakespeare builds up an atmosphere of dramatic tension on stage and between the characters.

Key points

Look for at least 6 of these and mark each out of 4.

- It is night in the castle courtyard. Lady Macbeth waits anxiously for her husband who is 'above', killing the king. Immediately, we should be aware that even the steely Lady Macbeth – 'Come to my woman's breasts and take my milk for gall' – is nervous, a reflection that she is human. To calm her nerves, she has been drinking, 'That which hath made them drunk hath made me bold'. We also find out that she has drugged the drinks of the king's grooms to make the murder easier.

- Like all of us when we know that we are doing wrong our conscience makes us much more aware of the situation around us because we are afraid of being caught. Lady Macbeth is speaking quietly, almost waiting in a corner of the stage, trying to be an inconspicuous as possible. The murder takes place off stage. Shakespeare is more interested in the atmosphere and the impact on the two major characters than on a bloody and savage action scene.

- Also remember the restrictions of Shakespeare's theatre. The productions took place in the daytime. This scene is at night. Night and blackness are symbolic of evil – the right time to commit this dreadful deed. Shakespeare had no sophisticated lighting; he had to create the atmosphere by the use of words and images. Straight away, to create the feeling among the audience that they might be caught, she says that she hears noises, 'Hark!'. But it is nothing, 'Peace' – just an owl shrieking. The audience now know that it is night.

- Macbeth emerges out of the darkness making a loud noise. This shocks Lady Macbeth – he should not be attracting attention – and she is afraid that something has happened. Note 'He could not miss 'em' when she refers to her husband and the daggers she has left. Does this suggest she doubts his capability to do the job properly?

- Macbeth is carrying the bloody daggers. He is shocked and 'rambling' – not in control at all. This is a big contrast to the 'brave Macbeth' we have seen earlier. His nervousness ('Did not you speak?') makes Lady Macbeth nervous, too, and the jerky nature of their responses suggests that their own speech, echoing in the empty courtyard, terrifies them in the light of what they have done.

- Macbeth sees the blood on his hands and starts to talk about his crime. They are 'hangman's hands'; he reflects on religion, explaining that the grooms were praying and he could not finish the prayer with 'Amen'. Throughout the play the image of 'blood' reinforces the evil of the story. The word appears in many of the speeches. He washes the blood away in this scene – 'wash this filthy witness' – but he cannot wash away the crime. In an ironic reflection later on, Lady Macbeth in her madness cannot clean the blood from her hands.

- Another image continued throughout the play is one of sleep. Macbeth thinks he has 'murdered sleep' because of his deed. Remember that the Elizabethans believed in the divine right of kings; a king was directly appointed by God. So in killing a king the murder directly offended God. Macbeth never rests again. Lady Macbeth sleeps in her madness but cannot rest – she sleepwalks.

- Lady Macbeth is shocked by the fact her husband has brought the daggers with him. They are incriminating evidence, and the blood on his hands is a 'filthy witness'. She has to shout at him, almost like a naughty child – 'Infirm of purpose'. The 'brave' Macbeth refuses to return to the murder scene and it is left to Lady Macbeth to take control and place the daggers in the hands of the grooms to incriminate them: 'Give me the daggers. The sleeping and the dead are but as pictures'. She even makes an evil joke by punning on 'gilt' and 'guild' in her speech – as if she is trying to cover up her fear.

- To increase the tension, a knocking is heard on the castle gates just as she goes. The sound will wake everyone else and the crime will be discovered. The audience wants to know: will they manage to get the daggers back, wash the blood from their bodies and change their clothes before they have to greet the people?

- Macbeth stands motionless looking at the blood on his hands as the knocking continues. When Lady Macbeth returns to find him still standing there; her hands are bloody – of 'your colour' – but she is not as cowardly as her warrior husband, 'I shame/To wear a heart so white'. She is the one to organise her husband again; as the knocking continues she gives him strict instructions to change his clothes, and the castle awakes. The audience is now ready to see how the murder is discovered and its consequences.

Checklist for Assessing Written Expression

Level 4	Yes	No
Ideas clearly expressed.		
Paragraphs – organised ideas		
Punctuation to separate sentences generally accurate		
Spelling of simple words accurate		
Handwriting clear and legible		

Level 5	Yes	No
Ideas clearly expressed.		
Wide vocabulary, precise use of words		
Simple and complex sentences used – made into paragraphs		
Variety of punctuation – apostrophes and commas used correctly		
Spelling words – complex regular patterns		
Handwriting – clear, legible, fluent		

Level 6	Yes	No
Ideas clearly expressed with a sense of purpose		
A varied vocabulary used – appropriate language expressed in simple and complex sentences – good paragraphing		
Spelling accurate – some difficult words still incorrect		
Range of punctuation used – some more difficult forms		
Handwriting fluent and legible		

Level 7	Yes	No
Confidently expressed ideas – words chosen are appropriate		
Appropriate style is matched by appropriate language		
Accurate grammar and punctuation – being consciously used for effect		
Correct paragraphing and punctuation		
Spelling correct of irregular words		

If your child needs more practice in Shakespeare, use the WHSmith Key Stage 3 English Revision Guide.

The chart below will give an indication of performance in the combined English tests and provide a National Curriculum level.

Because the exam criteria for marking will change from year to year, dependent on the difficulty of the test and the students involved, it is impossible to make this process exact.

Total the marks which have been given for both papers. The score will be out of 100.

- Paper 1 is marked out of 60
- Paper 2 is marked out of 40

Combined score of Papers 1 and 2	Approximate National Curriculum Level
29 and below	Below Level 4
30 – 45	Level 4
46 – 60	Level 5
61 – 75	Level 6
76 – 85	Level 7
86 and above	Above Level 7

Those achieving above Level 7 could be taking a supplementary test paper – see pages 46 to 53. Those achieving below Level 4 should be taking a special paper. It is best to consult your child's teacher if this is the case.

Extension Paper

Who can take an Extension Paper?

Taking an extra Extension Paper in these tests gives students the opportunity to achieve Level 8 or to demonstrate exceptional performance. In order to do this, the Extension Paper assesses 'higher-order' reading and writing skills. The Extension Paper is therefore considerably more difficult in its choice of extracts for reading and in the tasks it sets.

Only students who gain a Level 7 in Papers 1 and 2 can be awarded a higher level for their performance in the Extension Paper. It is necessary to prove that the student can perform at Level 7 before attempting an Extension Paper.

Students who take the Extension Paper may be awarded a Level 8 or EP (Exceptional Performance).

How is it different from the other test papers?

An Extension Paper has two questions:

- One question which asks students to read and compare two passages of prose – one written in the twentieth century and one written before this time.

- The second question asks students to write 200 to 300 words on a choice of topics, either giving their views or writing a narrative (story) or a description.

Extension Paper

The test is **1 hour 30 minutes** long.

You should answer both questions. Spend about 45 minutes on each.

Your ability to understand what you read and to express your ideas in writing will be assessed in this paper.

Check your work carefully.

Read the two passages (**A and B**) on pages 47 and 48 which use the weather conditions to create an effect.

Then answer the questions which follow.

You will be asked to write about both of the passages.

Passage A

This extract is from Great Expectations, *a novel by Charles Dickens. Pip, the young boy in the story, has stolen some food, including a pork-pie, in order to help an escaped convict who is hiding in the marshes.*

It was a rimy* morning, and very damp. I had seen the damp lying on the outside of my little window, as if some goblin had been crying here all night, and using the window for a pocket handkerchief. Now I saw the damp lying on the bare hedges and spare grass, like a coarser sort of spiders' webs; hanging itself from twig and blade to blade. On every rail and gate, wet lay clammy, and the marsh mist was so thick that the wooden finger on the post directing people to our village – a direction which they never accepted, for they never came there – was invisible to me until I was quite close under it. Then, as I looked up at it, while it dripped, it seemed to my oppressed conscience like a phantom devoting me to the Hulks.*

The mist was heavier yet when I got out upon the marshes, so that instead of my running at everything, everything seemed to run at me. This was very disagreeable to a guilty mind. The gates and dykes and banks came bursting at me through the mist, as if they cried plainly as could be: 'A boy with Somebody-else's pork-pie! Stop him!'

The cattle came upon me with like suddenness, staring out of their eyes, and steaming out of their nostrils. 'Holloa, young thief!' One black ox, with a white cravat on – who even had to my awakened conscience something of a clerical air – fixed me so obstinately with his eyes, and moved his blunt head round in such an accusatory manner as I moved round, that I blubbered out to him: 'I couldn't help it, sir! It wasn't for myself I took it!' Upon which he put down his head, blew a cloud of smoke out of his nose, and vanished with a kick-up of his hind-legs and a flourish of his tail.

* rimy – frosty

* Hulks – ships used to transport prisoners to Australia in the nineteenth century.

Passage B

This extract is from A High Wind in Jamaica, *a novel by Richard Hughes. In this extract the Thornton family, living on a plantation, experience a hurricane.*

Emily tried to fix her interest on every least detail of the scene around her – to count the slats in the shutters, any least detail that was *outward*. So it was that for the first time she really began to notice the weather.

The wind by now was more than redoubled. The shutters were bulging as if tired elephants were leaning against them, and Father was trying to tie the fastening with his handkerchief. But to push against the wind was like trying to push against rock. The handkerchief, shutters, everything burst: the rain poured in like the sea into a sinking ship, the wind occupied the room, snatching the pictures from the wall, sweeping the table bare. Through the gaping frames the lightning-lit scene without was visible. The creepers, which before had looked like cobwebs, now streamed up into the sky like new-combed hair. Bushes were lying flat, laid back on the ground as close as a rabbit lays back his ears. Branches were leaping about loose in the sky. The huts were clean gone, and the farm workers crawling on their stomachs across the compound to gain the shelter of the house. The bouncing rain seemed to cover the ground with a white smoke. One boy began to roll away: his mother, forgetting caution, rose to her feet: and immediately the fat old beldam* was blown clean away, bowling across fields and hedgerows like someone in a funny fairy story, till she fetched up against a wall and was pinned there unable to move. But the others managed to reach the house and soon could be heard in the cellar beneath.

Moreover, the very floor began to ripple, as a loose carpet will ripple on a gusty day: in opening the cellar door the farm workers had let the wind in, and now for some time they could not shut it again. The wind, to push against, was more like a solid block than a current of air.

* beldam – an ancient word meaning 'ugly old woman'.

Questions

Answer Question 1 and Question 2.

Question 1

Compare the way the writers have described and used the weather in these extracts.

You should consider:

- The writers' choice of detail and language.

- The feelings and attitudes of the writers towards their subject.

- How they use the description of weather to highlight other things, e.g. character.

- Which piece you think is more effective and why.

Question 2

Choose **one** of the following.

Concentrate on the quality of your writing. You will also be assessed on your use of spelling, grammar and punctuation, and the way you express your ideas.

Write about 200 to 300 words.

a) Write a description of extreme weather conditions and the effect they have on people and places.

Concentrate on using language effectively to create the atmosphere.

The events you describe can be real or imagined.

OR

b) It is believed that the climate of an area can often affect the character of the people who live there, e.g. people who live in hot climates can be 'hot-tempered'; people who live in cold climates can be more reserved. Write a speech to be delivered before your class which argues for or against this view.

Use an appropriate style for a speech and an argument.

Use examples to back up your point of view.

Use pages 50–51 for your notes.

Questions 1 and 2

Here are some features to look for in assessment:

Objectives for assessment

- To show an understanding and appreciation of ideas and themes in literature.

- To understand how writers use language effects, the structure of sentences and paragraphs and presentational devices to achieve specific effects.

- To interpret a text and to support opinions by reference to these views.

Content of answers

- Make reference to the writers' choice of words and expressions and their effectiveness – how they work. Consider Dickens' delicate image of the goblin to explain the lightness of the mist which Pip sees outside or the strength of Hughes' wind, 'like pushing against a rock'.

- Be aware of figurative language – similes, metaphors, personification – and be able to explain how this makes the text more effective. Both authors use personification for different reasons. Dickens makes everything that Pip sees come alive because it is a reflection of his guilty conscience for becoming a thief. The very world seems to know of his guilt and is reprimanding him. The weather enables this to happen – the mysterious fog ensure the scene is shifting all the time. He creates almost a dream world – for Pip it is closer to a nightmare. The weather is used by Dickens as a reflection of the state of mind of the character. Hughes uses personification to show that the world as we know it is out of control – the hurricane has taken over as a physical force and human beings are useless to fight it.

- Show awareness and understanding of the particular written form of the extract and the stylistic features associated with it. Dickens uses almost a comic style as everything that emerges from the mist is eccentric – down to the ox compared to a vicar. But to Pip, as a young child, this is deadly serious. Again, Dickens is able to give us an impression of the mind of a young child through his style – consider the speech in the passage.

- Be able to analyse and compare the mood of the passages. The moods of the two passages are very different. Dickens uses the weather to create a realistic effect of the guilty conscience of a young child – almost a fantasy. Hughes creates an intensely vivid description appealing to our senses. There is something dispassionate about the reaction to people, however. This passage is about the effects of the weather – in times of life and death, the reaction to others may not seem so important as your own survival.

- Compare the different viewpoints. Note the passage is written in the first person – from the point of view of the child. Hughes writes in the third person, but there is a sense that he is involved in some way: the voice could almost be that of someone involved. All the senses are appealed to, which creates the overall impression of the effect of the hurricane.

Mark scheme – Questions 1 and 2

Features	Level
• Students' understanding of both texts is reasonably secure, and they appreciate some of the differences between them but their comparisons are not very clear or do not focus on the key points. • They use some quotations to support their comments but these are not explored in any detail and opinions expressed about their impressions of the passages are not always fully explained. • They recognise some literary features but explanations of the effects may be limited. • Their answers tend to be based on description of the content of the texts and they may ignore or misinterpret more difficult ideas and imagery.	Below Level 8
• Students recognise the essential differences in the writers' descriptions and in their feelings towards their subjects. • They note how Dickens' language describing the weather is used to reflect the feelings and conscience of the small boy and how Hughes' imagery creates a description appealing to all our senses. • They use relevant quotation and reference to the texts and justify and expand their comments, and support their impressions of the texts with appropriate reasons. • There is some understanding of literary techniques and the effects achieved by their use.	Level 8
• Students demonstrate a confident and detailed understanding of the ways in which the ideas in texts are presented. • Quotations and textual references are precisely selected to justify comment and used to explore the differences both in the writers' views of their subjects and the techniques used to express them. • Pupils discuss complex ideas and imagery effectively, providing a focused and convincing answer to the question.	Exceptional Performance